T0157487

Surviving by the Grace of God

Mary E.D. Norris

authorHOUSE®

AuthorHouse™
1663 Liberty Drive
Bloomington, IN 47403
www.authorhouse.com
Phone: 1 (800) 839-8640

© 2015 Mary Norris. All rights reserved.

No part of this book may be reproduced, stored in a retrieval system, or transmitted by any means without the written permission of the author.

Published by AuthorHouse   11/10/2015

ISBN: 978-1-5049-5978-0 (sc)
ISBN: 978-1-5049-5976-6 (e)

Print information available on the last page.

Any people depicted in stock imagery provided by Thinkstock are models, and such images are being used for illustrative purposes only. Certain stock imagery © Thinkstock.

This book is printed on acid-free paper.

Because of the dynamic nature of the Internet, any web addresses or links contained in this book may have changed since publication and may no longer be valid. The views expressed in this work are solely those of the author and do not necessarily reflect the views of the publisher, and the publisher hereby disclaims any responsibility for them.

KJV
Scripture quotations marked KJV are from the Holy Bible, King James Version (Authorized Version). First published in 1611. Quoted from the KJV Classic Reference Bible, Copyright © 1983 by The Zondervan Corporation.

Mary Norris shares the pain and heartache of losing a grandson, a husband and four children. God blessed her by leaving her with one child in her life, and she thanks the Lord daily for him. God's grace and love has been sufficient to carry her through her life and any situation she may face. If you believe and trust in the Lord he will carry you too. Jesus came to heal the brokenhearted, and he will if you will allow him to.

CHAPTER 1

The Beginning

1940 - 1963

In 1940 my mama Betty Horne and my daddy John Dowless got married in a little town called Dublin, North Carolina. They stayed with my dad's parents for the first year. Then they had their first son Purlie and Daddy and Mama move to Elizabethtown, North Carolina. My daddy went to work for Mr Rich Johnson as a sharecropper. Back then they raised corn, tobacco, peanuts, and cotton. After all the crops were harvested and sold daddy would get his part for his year of work. Everything was worked with mules and horses working from sun up to sun down. In 1943 my brother Jimmy was born. As time went on my daddy was out in the fields plowing and praying. He asked the Lord to send him a little girl he wanted one so bad, and on May 9th, 1945 God sent him what he asked for, a nine pound baby girl and mama named me Mary Estelle after her Mother.

Back then you raised your own meat, we had cows, hogs, chickens, and goats from these animals is how we got our milk and eggs. What milk and eggs we couldn't use daddy would sell. He would take corn to the grist mill to have ground into corn meal and grits. Things were tough by the time I was 5 years old. Daddy would borrow $10 a week from the landlord to buy sugar, flour and things you couldn't grow in the garden. We didn't have a refrigerator or a washing machine. Daddy would heat water in a large pot and we would wash clothes on the scrub board. We had a ice box that sat on the front porch and the Ice man would come by once a week and Mama would buy a block of ice that would last for about 3 days.At the time we didn't have a car so Daddy would take the mule and wagon and go to town about a mile away to get a few groceries we had to have. We had a wood heater in the winter Daddy would take my two brothers

1

and me and we would go cut wood with a cross cut saw. They would cut it and I would stack it on the wagon.

In 1951 another brother was born and they named him Clarence. I was 6 years old at the time he was born and Mamas health wasn't good. Her nerves were so bad she would cry for days and Daddy would have to go get the doctor to come out and give her a shot, and then she would sleep for 2 days, so here I am at 6 years old changing and washing diapers on the scrub board for my brother. The tenant house we lived in was in bad shape, there were cracks in the floor. We would get so bored at times we would take pieces of tobacco twine and tie it around a grain of corn and put it through the cracks to pick on the chickens under the house.

At Christmas time we would get one toy, one apple and one orange. There was a lady that had a little store about a 1/2 mile from our house and she sold drinks or sodas as some called them. If you saved up enough Dr. Pepper caps you could trade them in for a Dr Pepper doll. So she saved the caps, you would've thought i owned the world when she gave me that doll. Back then you didn't get toys during the year only at Christmas.

Mama and Daddy's faith was so strong in the Lord, and they believed and had no doubt that he would take care of us. When the weather allowed we walked 1 1/2 miles to church on Sunday mornings. Once in awhile someone we knew would come along and pick us up and take us on to our church then they would go on to theirs. The year came when we finally got a washing machine and we thought God is good. In 1956 Daddy had a bumper crop and was able to buy mama a refrigerator and the family a car. I felt so blessed and thankful my parents raised me in a Christian home.

In 1957 we moved to White Oak, North Carolina about 7 miles from where we were living before. It was owned by the same landlord. And then here came another brother they named Charles. Now I have two brothers older than me and two younger than me. I had to grow up fast. I was learning how to cook and helping Mama take care of my two younger brothers. At age12 it was like I was their second mama. At the age of 15 I was in the 9th grade and started taking home economics classes and was making beautiful biscuits. From grade 9 - 12 I worked in the lunchroom washing dishes during recess to pay for our lunches. When I was in the 12th grade and it was time to buy my class ring daddy sold a wagon load of corn to pay for my ring. I was so proud of it. At that time in 1963 class rings were only $27.50. I can remember that day as if it was yesterday. I went to work shortly after graduating for a man at his grill he also owned the filling station next door that my brother Jimmy work at. He had a car so we worked the same hours so we could ride back and forth together to work.

CHAPTER 2

My True Love

In September 1963 I met the " Love of My Life " Herman Norris. After the third date I found out he had been married before with two children. Ray was 4 and Kay was 2 and he had custody of them. After we had been dating for 6 months Herman asked me to marry him. I told him yes, but only if I could take the children and raise them as my own because it was a package deal. I couldn't love him and not love them. He told me it would be an honor. So I married into a ready-made family and I don't regret one minute of it.

7 months later I gave birth to a 6 pd. 12 ounce little girl that was born prematurely. I had fallen down the door steps and started bleeding, which caused me to go into labor 2 months early. On that day I understood God's plan for this. I found out later if I hadn't had her when I did she wouldn't have lived, the umbilical cord was wrapped around her neck and she had already turned purple. We named her Teresa Lynn, she turned out to be a very happy and healthy baby. When she turned 2 we moved to South Hill, Virginia to manage a restaurant for a year until they sold out to Greyhound Bus Company then we moved back to Fayetteville, North Carolina and Herman went to work painting houses for a housing development. In November 1967 Robert was born and then in 1971 Ricky was born. We were blessed with 5 beautiful healthy children and we thanked God each day.

When I had been working at Dunkin Donuts for about 5 1/2 years Herman and I decided to go into the Catering Service. The Lions Club was looking for someone to cook and serve for them once a week. They had their own building and kitchen. They rented to different groups and clubs weekly such as the Lady Lions, the Rotary Club, and the Kiwanis Club. We would also cater to other groups and parties. In June 1978 we had been with them about 6 years when I found out I had to have surgery. The weekend before my surgery our oldest daughter Kay wanted to take her brothers and sister to a lake near Fort Bragg for a picnic. All of them went but Ray....

CHAPTER 3

The Wreck

My daughter Kay was married at the age of 16 and had a baby boy 11 months old named Lee. She wanted to take her siblings on a picnic at a lake near Ft. Bragg North Carolina. They went to the picnic and her husband Lamar was drinking. On the way back home they got into an argument. He ran off the road and jerked the car back on the road, hit a median and the car shot up in the air 10-12 feet hitting a tree. They said bodies were flying everywhere. Back then they didn't have to have seatbelts, they clocked him going 90 mph. Herman and I were sitting on the front porch and heard sirens going off one right after the other. It was only a 1/2 mile (as the crow flies) from our home. I told Herman something terrible has happened.

About 30 minutes later I received a phone call from Cape Fear Valley Hospital saying there had been an accident and they may have to admit my son Robert. I was so shocked I don't even remember the drive to the hospital. When we got to the hospital they wouldn't let us see any of them because they were working on their injuries, I knew then just how terrible this was. We went outside the emergency room because it was crowded. As we were standing outside a black lady came up to me and said honey, the Lord told me to come to the hospital, she said she didn't know why but when she seen me standing there she knew I was the reason she was there. God had sent her there to pray for me and my family.

I had strayed and gotten out from under the umbrella of the protection of the Lord. I learned he loved me so much that he sent reinforcements to help me for I did not know what I was facing. I told her my children have been in a serious accident, and she laid her hands on my head and prayed for me and my family. When she started, it felt like warm honey was pouring from my head and went over my entire body. At the time I didn't understand what was happening. God had put me in a semi - shock state of mind so I would be able to withstand what I was about to face. A nurse came out and told us the doctor wanted to talk to us, my body felt numb as they let us into the conference room and began telling us about the wreck and what was happening....

Lamar 22 our son in law had broken his jaw bone and he had tubes running everywhere. Kay 16 our oldest daughter had a deep long gash a hairs width from her jugular vein. Robert 11 had a severe head concussion. They had found him in the ditch and had to put a stick in his mouth to keep him from chewing his tongue. Teresa 14 was the only one who could tell them who to call, and she had been thrown through the back window of the car. She had broken her glasses and she was in shock. My youngest Ricky 7 they were giving him blood because he was bleeding internally. I asked the doctor about our 11 month old grandson Lee, he said he didn't survive and had died from the blow to the back of the head where he had hit the dashboard. I was thinking, this is a nightmare God, no parent should have to go through so much pain at one time with every child in their family. The doctor finally allowed us to go see them but we had to be quiet and try to keep them as quiet as possible.

They put Kay and her husband on one floor. Teresa and Robert on another floor across the hall from each other. Ricky was put in intensive care. The nurse had asked us to stay gathered in one of the children's room so if they needed to contact us they would know where to find us. So we chose Roberts room because he had to be kept awake because of his head trauma.

CHAPTER 4

CB Radio Club & Ft. Bragg

At the time we belonged to a CB Radio Club and the news had gotten out about the wreck and Ricky needing blood, he had hit a tree and knocked one of his kidneys completely loose inside, they had found it when they done the exploratory surgery on him. The nurse came and said one of us needed to go to the downstairs lobby, because it was full of people wanting to donate blood and to find out how the children were doing. They had taken 25 pints from all these people who wanted to so desperately help their friends. But they had to stop accepting donations because after so long the blood would be no good. So Herman went down to tell the CB Club thank you and to tell them all the donations were greatly appreciated. And they could not accept any more blood at this time.

Meanwhile they were preparing to air - lift Ricky to a hospital in Chapel Hill, North Carolina. All the helicopters at Cape Fear Valley Hospital were in flight. Our next door neighbor was high in rank at Ft. Bragg Army Base in North Carolina and pulled some strings and they allowed Cape Fear Valley to use one of the Army's helicopters to transport Ricky to Chapel Hill. From Robert's room you could see the landing pad for the helicopter. We were watching out the window and Robert wanted to know what was going on out there, we tried to smooth it over because he was going in and out and we had to keep him awake. So we finally had to tell him what was going on. That didn't go very well at all with him. They got ready to load Ricky and had to unload him and bring him back, they had lost him. After they revived him they reloaded him again and air - lifted him to Chapel Hill Hospital. I was in a mess, I didn't know whether to go with Ricky or stay. The doctor told me to stay there, the other children need you here. He told me the nurses at Chapel Hill would keep me informed on what was going on with Ricky. So I stayed, and my heart filled with such pain at not being able to be at both places at once.

CHAPTER 5

Anger, Hurt, Pain and Relief

I was so angry, so hurt, I felt like screaming. My intentions were to go to my son in laws room and pull every tube out of him. Kill him if I could, make him suffer for the pain he had cause my whole family. When I got 3 ft. from his bed, I froze in my tracks and I know it was God who stopped me. I couldn't say or do anything. Lamar ask me " did you see my car? " that's all he asked me about was his car. I thought here is a person so self - centered, no remorse for what he had caused. I don't know if it was an Angel or God who carried me out of his room. As Kay and Lamar were on the mend they were released from the hospital. They had my grandsons funeral but I couldn't go because Robert and Teresa we're being released and we had to go to Chapel Hill to check on Ricky. We were driving back and forth every other day. On the days we couldn't go the nurses would call and tell us how he was doing that day. We were trying to work during all of this we still had to pay bills.

Infection had begun to set in from the loss of the kidney and they put Ricky on a dialysis machine to try to purify his blood. The infection had gotten so bad nothing else could be done. After 18 days the doctor said there was no brain activity. Then came the question no parent should have to answer.... The doctor asked us if we wanted to turn off the machine? I begged the Lord to let him live, take me instead, but it didn't happen. That was my 7 year old baby.

But I realized later that God doesn't make deals or mistakes. Not knowing that God had a plan, it seemed so strange that 8 months before the accident it came to me that Herman and I needed to buy cemetery plots. So I called Cumberland Memorial Gardens. A man came out and talked to us about what they had and the prices. I wanted to be buried where they had someone to keep the cemetery clean, because I was thinking once your children grow up, get married and go in different directions it's hard for them to get back to keep them clean. So we decided to get the two plots and when you buy two you got a third free for one of your children if they needed it before they reached the age of 18. Not knowing 8 months later we would be burying our 7 year old son. I know God had his hand in it, for he knows the future.

The principal at the school Ricky went to ask each student to bring $1 to school to donate for the expenses of Ricky's funeral. His teacher gave us a check for $1,000, Lord what a blessing that was. Lamar called me and asked if he could come to the funeral. I told him that grave yard wasn't big enough for me and him both. I was so exhausted and reality was setting in, this was a nightmare no parent should have to endure.

CHAPTER 6

The Next Year

We still had Robert and Teresa at home, Ray the oldest wasn't in the accident. He had a place he stayed at with a friend. We picked glass out of Teresa's hair, face and body for weeks where she had broken her glasses, and from where she had flown through the back glass of the car. Robert had several large places on his head and temple that came around between his eye and ear. I would lay him on the counter at the kitchen sink and wash his hair and clean the wounds on the side of his face. I smile when I think back of the time after he was healed how he still wanted me to wash his hair, he said it felt good. I think I spoiled him... then I stop and think after all this heartache...WHY NOT?

The next year was so tough. I was so depressed, I prayed for the school bus to hurry and come so I could go back to bed. Herman had been drinking before but now it was worse. What time he wasn't working or sleeping he was drinking.

A year after the accident we had some friends Gary and his wife Carol they lived in Florida called, and said they were coming by they were in town visiting. They came and we found out that he had got saved and living for the Lord. That night Herman drank and drank and it was as if he were drinking water he wasn't getting drunk. Gary and Carol were ministering to him, all of a sudden Herman got up and said Gary and I would be back in a little while. They stayed gone for about an hour, when they got back home and Herman said you will never believe where I have been? I said ok, where have you been? He said while he was sitting at our kitchen table he saw a huge Angel hovering over us and it scared the devil out of him. He had gone to Lamar's, knocked on the door and Lamar's Daddy answered. Herman ask to speak to Lamar and he came to the door with a look on his face as if to say " this is my last night on earth." Herman told him " I have laid awake for one year trying to figure out a way to kill you and get away with it." Herman said to him, now I ask you to forgive me so I can live in peace. Lamar ask Him to forgive him for putting him through all the torture and loss he had caused our family. And from that night forward Herman Norris was a changed man.

He went from having a Beer in his hands to having a Bible in his hands. It didn't take me long to get my life right with the Lord. I called Lamar over to talk with him. I told him the Lord told me if I don't forgive you I would never get the chance to go and see my son and grandson. So I asked him to forgive me, and I ministered him and won him to the Lord. Kay was trying to make the marriage work but she couldn't, he was in Georgia last time I heard from him.

CHAPTER 7

The Change In Our Lives

I didn't know what God was up to, but I knew something was going on inside of Herman. It was like God was giving him a crash course of the Bible. He ate it, he drank it, he slept it. He wasn't content unless he was in the word In January of 1980 he said the Lord had called him to preach. I thought to myself, I can't be a preacher's wife! But I accepted the fact that we were one in the eyes of God. All I know is I was enjoying the peace in our home.

In February we put our house on the market for sale. At that time we knew we were moving to Garland, North Carolina where Herman was raised and his family lived. At the time houses weren't selling fast. In one month the house was sold and we had to move. There was a lady and she had an old house and she wanted him to start a church, we felt this was what God was leading us to do. He started preaching, and God was truly blessing. In 1984 I started a four year Bible course from Rhema Correspondence Bible School through Kenneth Hagin Ministries. The church was growing and doing well, and we started building the new church.

We had a piano player, but Robert at the age of 15 had the greatest desire to play. He had taken a chorus class in school but no music lessons. During church one Sunday Robert asked his daddy to anoint his hands, and ask God to give him the gift of playing the piano. His daddy anointed his hands with oil and prayed over them, and ask God to anoint him to sing and play for the Glory of God. Robert went to the piano and sat down and fumbled around a little bit, and started playing like he had played all his life. The more he played the more the Lord anointed him. And as of this day we are praying for the finances for him to make a CD, and it is coming sooner than we think. God will do it in HIS time not ours.

CHAPTER 8

Herman Norris

1993

In 1993 Herman was strong in the Lord. He preached under a heavy anointing. It was not cut and dry, he didn't water it down so the people would like him. He preached as if it didn't matter what came of his words.

He started having asthma attacks now and then. This was something that ran in his family, his sister has severe asthma. And in May of 1993 he was diagnosed with COPD. When he was a painter he was using lead paint, he painted for a grocery store chain. They would paint at night when the stores were closed. They were locked in so they inhaled all of those paint fumes. In January 1995 he was diagnosed with lung cancer. We prayed, the church prayed and in May we were sitting on our front porch and while he was reading the newspaper a butterfly landed on it. One of the most beautiful and graceful butterflies I had ever seen, it sat there for a good 3 minutes. I said to Herman this butterfly is bringing a message to us, neither of us said anything we just quietly sat there, a little while later we went back inside. 2 hours later the Lord told me he was going to take Herman home but didn't tell me when.

I saw him so weak at times that he would hold on to the pulpit to stay standing up. He preached under the annointing and after he would finish the service he would become as weak as a dishcloth. In September he told me unless the Lord intervenes he wouldn't be here for Thanksgiving. I called the doctor and made an appointment to talk with him. I needed to know what to expect. The doctor told me that he would give him until Thanksgiving. I knew then that things were lining up for Herman now. By this time he was on oxygen 24 hours a day, and in a lot of pain. He didn't want me out of his sight. I couldn't deal with it, all I could do was ask the

Lord not to let him suffer. I got a baby monitor and put it in his room and the other in the living room, when he would fall asleep I would slip out of his room but could still hear him.

The Lord gave me Isaiah 54 to read, I would read it over and over but only understanding part of it. All I knew was the Lord would be my husband, and he would give me children I didn't bare. As the days got shorter Herman would talk to me and tell me what a good woman I was. He would say I would buy you the moon if I could. The night before he went to heaven our oldest son Ray went into his dads room and shut the door and two hours later came out. I have no idea what they said to each other that night and I never asked.

The next morning I couldn't understand what Herman was trying to tell me. I couldn't deal with this, I laid my hands on his chest and prayed Lord don't let him suffer, I release his spirit into your bosom and allow him to go in peace. And as God as my witness it was like a neon light went around the bed three times. I left out and Robert went in and seen his breathing pattern had changed. The nurse came and told us if there was anything we wanted to say to him we needed to do it, because it was just a matter of time. So we all went in and said our goodbyes. I told him it was okay if he wanted to go home now and that I would be okay. At that moment he drew his last breath and graduated to heaven. Sometimes we are selfish and want to keep our a loved ones here with us. It was a relief to turn him loose because I had watched him suffer for 17 months. There were times when he was in so much pain he would beg the Lord to just go ahead and take him home. I couldn't cry at the time, for I knew once his feet hit the Streets of Gold there was no more pain. I knew one day I would join him and the rest of my family and loved ones.

As time went on I realized my spiritual leader, my prayer partner and my husband wasn't there anymore. So I had to go back to (Isaiah 54:5)... for the maker is thy husband; the LORD of hosts is his name; and the Redeemer the Holy One of Israel; the God of the whole earth shall be called.

And believe me I had to really do some calling on the Lord now.

CHAPTER 9

Mary Norris

Let's talk about me in this chapter. I had so much pain, hurt, anger, and loss in my life but I knew the Lord was on my side, I would make it......

My body had started falling apart. I was diagnosed with fibromyalgia, a muscle disease. I think it came from the stress I had been under from the accident and the 17 months with Herman's cancer. My hips hurt so bad, I would have to take both hands and put under my hips to turn my body over on my side. There are 18 places in the body that this disease can attack. Between the Lord first, and then the doctors it was finally under control, so I could go back to work there was no income coming in at home. I struggled through it but I knew my God was my provider. He always showed up on time, regardless of the pain " The Joy of the Lord is my Strength"

I was still having health problems. My heart would start beating twice as fast as it should, then it would return to normal. About a year later I was working at a grill and it started and hadn't stopped after an hour, it was taking a toll on my body. It was beating 183 times a minute. They called the rescue squad and they gave me five baby aspirin, it didn't seem to help. By the time they got me to the hospital and they checked me out, and they hooked me to the machines it still hadn't slowed back to normal. The doctor said they were going to stop my heart and then restart it again. I thought to myself.... No.... No.... No.... I started praying " Lord this is a good opportunity to show yourself."

The doctor had gone to get the medicine to inject into my IV to stop my heart, and this little nurse came running into my room all excited saying we got it, we got it. I looked up at the machine and saw on the monitor that it had changed over and went back to normal. The doctor came in and said " I know what happened, we scared it out of her." I laughed and told the doctor, "No you don't know in whom I trust, it was God that did this." So I got dressed and went home giving God the Glory.

In December 2003, I came down with double pneumonia. I was airlifted from Bladen County Hospital in Elizabethtown North Carolina to New Hanover Medical Center in Wilmington North Carolina. I spent 11 days in intensive care, and five days on the main floor. I remember when I got to New Hanover hospital, the nurses told the children not to ask me any questions because it was bringing my oxygen level down to low when I tried to talk, and they were pushing my oxygen level to the limit so I could breathe. Things turned out for the worse, I don't know what was happening in the natural, but I remember what happened in the spirit realm. I saw myself in a room, it was so bright it was like a light shining on ice. I asked the Lord, where am I? He told me that this was a holding room I was in, and I asked him, what is the holding room? He said I have placed you here so Satan can't touch you. He asked me, Do you want to go home? He was talking about (Heaven). I told him I wanted to go, but I wanted to spend one more Christmas with my children.

Kay came to see me the next morning and ask the nurse what happened last night mom wasn't like this? The nurse told her I had a bad night. Later I remembered hearing a nurse telling me breathe Mrs. Norris breathe. A few days later I started recognizing my family, I wanted to go home for Christmas to spend it with my children, but the doctor kept me one more day with the understanding that someone would have to stay with me. I was so weak I couldn't take care of myself. So my son and his wife stayed with me for a week until they knew I could take care of myself. Then we had Christmas, God is so Good, Satan has lost again. He thought for sure he had me, but God has the last say in this matter.

The doctor did tell me when I got to feeling better they would fix my heart, because during the time I was in the hospital I had another attack of my heart beating too fast. I did go back and they checked my heart out and found a dead place in the wall of one of the chambers. The doctor went in and around the dead place and went in each chamber and sped up my heart. They went from chamber to chamber and all of them worked fine, God had worked out another situation for me with the doctors help. In 2006 I had to have a stint put in on the back side of my heart, the stint seems to be doing fine.

I understand the poem "Footprints in the Sand." I can see the one set of footprints, for he has carried me so many times, him knowing I couldn't walk on my own, it is good that we don't know what the future holds, for there are many things our minds couldn't handle in this life. He still carries me through every day.

In 2009 things didn't feel right in my chest, so I made an appointment with the heart doctor. My appointment was at the Heart Center. The doctor went in with a catheter and found scar tissue was growing around the edge of the stint that was implanted in 2006. They would have to go in and clean the stint out and put a stint in the top and the bottom of the one I already had. They took me back to my room and told me they couldn't do this procedure at the Heart Center. It would have to be done at the hospital, and it couldn't be done that day because there were no beds available. So the nurse told me they would set up the appointment and let me know when, the nurse also told me when I use the bathroom and got dressed I could go home. The nurse had taken the IV out of my arm and had turned around to do some paperwork so I set up on the bed, and swung my legs off the bed, what I didn't realize was the bed was higher from the floor than I thought, and when I slid off the bed to the floor I landed so hard I broke my ankle in 3 places. They called for the Rescue Squad to come and take me to the hospital. I remember they tried to pull my ankle back in place, it was so painful I said "Lord help me Jesus" and I passed out. My son Robert was there and heard the driver tell them to sedate me heavily because it was going to be a rough ride for her. After that I don't remember anything.

Robert said I told him I was hungry, so he went and got a hamburger and fries for each of us. He said I ate my hamburger, and his but I let him have his fries. I don't remember eating any of it, I think it just funny to eat and not even remember what it tasted like.

The doctors put a soft cast on my ankle because I couldn't have surgery on it until they fix my heart. I had to wait 5 days before they could work on my heart, then I had to let them do surgery on my ankle. This is where the fun begins. I laid on the couch for 4 months waiting for it to heal so they could take just the boot off. Needless to say I wasn't a happy camper. There were many days and nights the Lord and I had long, long, long talks.

I was not used to being confined to. I have always been independent and took care of myself.

Robert had always been over protective of me, and this made him even worse and still is, but he knows where to draw the line. Of course I had rather he be that way, then not care at all. And believe me he is a blessing to me. He would take me to church, I had to use my wheelchair but I had to go to church, so he made sure I got there. I needed to have my spirit fed and I needed to hear him sing and play the piano, I am proud of what God is doing in Robert's life.

CHAPTER 10

Teresa Lynn Key

By this time God had called my daughter Teresa to be an intercessor (praying for others). She had become my best friend and my prayer partner. She was growing by leaps and bounds in the Lord. She was a threat to the devil and he wasn't going to lay down and play dead.

In 1997 she began to have headaches so severe they had to rush her to the hospital and that's when they found 6 aneurysm's in her head. She prayed and cried "Lord let me live to raise my two girls." They went after the most life-threatening one which was at the base of her skull and neck. All went well and in a month's time she was back to her normal self. The doctors didn't know if it came from the accident where she was thrown through the back glass or if she had inherited it from my side of the family. My mother had passed away from aneurysm in her head also.

In 2007 Teresa was a technology assistant at E.O Young Elementary School in Henderson, North Carolina. She knew something was wrong, but she wouldn't tell me she didn't want me to worry about her. She got to the point she would come home from school and wrap up in a homemade quilt I had made for her. She was going down fast health wise, the doctors were running test after test on her. The next step for her was to be tested for lupus. When they found out the problem was an aneurysm they stopped everything, because they found one that needed to be repaired before they did any more testing.

The doctors at Duke University Medical Center wanted to go in and put in a stint to strengthen the walls of the artery. She went in the hospital on August 22, 2007. I had planned to meet her there, but she wouldn't hear of it. She said mom "NO" I'm going to let them put the stint in and then go back home. We argued back and forth a little & I let her win. I think she saw everything went so well when they put my stints in that hers would go well too. Her husband Wayne was to keep me informed of how things were going. After the doctors went in and were near the aneurysm it burst and she had a massive stroke, and it was over she never made it back home. Here my daughter, my friend, my prayer partner was gone. My son in law's wife, my two granddaughters mama all gone.

There is a song by Dottie Rambo that has brought me a lot of comfort through the years, I would like to share with you. I hope it will give you the comfort it has always given me. This song helps me realize that God shared my husband and children with me to brighten my life, they still belong to him, I was only borrowing them. He holds the future for us all, he knows what is best for us all. We are like a piece of a puzzle and each day we are putting the puzzle together. But God already sees the finished product. He creates us and mold us into what he wants us to be.

He doesn't need our help, he needs our obedience.

Remind Me Dear Lord
By: Dottie Rambo

The things that I love and hold dear to my heart,
Are just borrowed they're not mine at all,
Jesus only let me use them to brighten my life
So remind me, remind me, Dear Lord.

Roll back the curtain of memory now and then
Show me where you brought me from
And where I could have been.
Remember I'm human, and humans forget

CHAPTER 11

Vivian Kay Jones

In 2010 I noticed my oldest daughter Kay was coughing a lot and she was hurting in her chest. I finally talked her into going to the doctor. She wouldn't tell me what the doctor had told her, she just said she had a chest cold. But my spirit didn't agree with that, I prayed and I prayed for her. She was a very private person, she wouldn't tell you about anything that was going on until she was ready to. Finally I told her that I knew that this had to do with more than just a chest cold. She knew the Lord would tell me if she didn't so she told me the doctor had diagnosed her with small cell lung cancer.

She had strayed from the Lord and gotten into drinking, but she had come back to the LORD and had been in church for about six months when she was diagnosed with cancer. The church annointed her and prayed over her for healing. We were very careful about what we confessed for Satan could hear all things. We believed with every ounce of faith we had and we put it in the Lords hands.

She went through the treatments, which made her so sick. She had beautiful long blonde hair, which had all fallen out, but she bought her a hat to wear to church. By this time there were big knots forming on her body and she was getting weaker and weaker causing her to loose more weight. By then she had gotten so weak she couldn't come to church. She finally told me one day the doctors said that they had done all they could do. I knew when they sent her home it was all in the Lord's hands and it was up to him from then on. When I couldn't go see her I would call and talk to her husband. He told me they had called Hospice in to care for her. I was glad in one sense, for it got to the point when I would call to check on her, I didn't feel like she was being taken care of the way she was supposed to be. When I would call I could tell by his voice had been drinking.

The day before Christmas I felt like I just had to go see her. Not knowing she was so weak she couldn't talk, she had wrote on a piece of paper "call mom." My grandson and I went to see her, I talked to her and prayed with her, it was breaking my heart she couldn't talk at all. That's the last time I saw her alive. Christmas day we had a bad ice storm and they had to take Kay to the hospital by rescue squad, and they had a time with all the ice, I had a small car and there was no way for me to get to her. I lived 22 miles from the hospital. She had went to be with the Lord on December 26th, 2010. A short while later the Lord spoke to me, and said I had no problem healing her on earth, but if I had she would have returned to her old ways. That made it easier for me to let go, knowing she had made it to heaven.

But how much Lord, can I take? I have two sons left! What now? I thought about what Paul was talking about in 2nd Corinthians 12... He said unto me. My grace is sufficient for thee: for my strength is made perfect in weakness. Most gladly therefore would I rather glory in my infinities, that the power of Christ may rest upon me. And I gladly began to quote the scriptures that would lift me up for I sure needed them.

1 Corinthians 10:13... there hath no temptation taken you but such as is common to man; but God is faithful, who will not suffer you to be tempted above that you are able; but with the temptation also make a way to escape, that you may be able to bear it.

Nehemiah 8:10... the joy of the Lord is my strength.

Isaiah 54... The Lord gave me children I didn't bare, and a place for them to live. For my Maker is my husband; the Lord of hosts is his name; and the Redeemer the Holy One of Israel; the God of the whole earth shall he be called.

I continued to quote the Scriptures until they got not only in my spirit but also in my mouth, there is a difference. I had been teaching Sunday school and that kept me in the word, and kept me going and I had my church family, and all of this helps me get stronger each day. The Lord allowed Isaiah 54, to come to pass in my life. I have all kinds and ages of children that I didn't bare but become a part of my life.

They call me "Nanny" or that is what my grandchildren call me. Even my pastor calls me "Mom." Regardless of all things I am a "blessed woman by the Grace of God." I am thankful for the children god blessed me with that I did not give birth to. They have brought forth love and joy to my life. Especially the hugs I receive from them that I can't receive from the ones who have already gone on to be with the Lord.

CHAPTER 12

Billy Ray Norris

By now I only have two sons left Ray the oldest and Robert. Ray was preaching and Robert was singing and playing the piano for our church. Not many mothers can say that all of their children knew and are with the Lord.

Then the day came when my oldest son Ray told me he didn't feel good. He told me his chest had been hurting him for a while now and he had started coughing, even at times when he was preaching. I finally convinced him to go and get checked out. I said to him "son I don't think I can handle losing another child." So I carried him to the hospital, and the next day the doctor sent him to another hospital to run more tests. They diagnosed him with small cell cancer Stage 3. The church prayed and prayed for him. He stayed by himself, and I know he wasn't taking care of himself. He and his wife had divorced years ago, and he had never remarried.

I had started taking him to his treatments and they would make him so sick. I told the nurse one day at one of his treatments to tell him to come and stay with me, so I can put some meat on his bones and she did. He finally came and stayed with me, but before he came the Lord told me he was going to take him home. So one day my sister in law and I went and bought him a shirt, tie and suit and put them in my closet. I had an insurance policy I had taken out on Ray when he was in his twenties, I took it out and went to the funeral home and made his arrangements. The church continued to pray for his healing, I knew what God had told me and I didn't want to dampen their spirit of faith. So I kept that part to myself.

After the first round of chemotherapy and radiation the doctor wasn't satisfied with the results. The doctor wanted him to take another round of chemo and radiation. Carol drove us to the doctor that day and on the way back home we stopped at the store, Ray said that he wanted something cold to drink, and he wanted to buy Carol and I a drink to say thank you for taking him. While I was in the store he asked Carol if he had to do any more treatments if he didn't want to, she told him "No" it was his decision to go or not to go. He told her he didn't want to go back anymore his body was tired and he wanted to rest. So when I got back in the car Carol told me what they had talked about and what Ray had decided to do, I won't say I was surprised because I knew he was tired, I turned around and looked at him and said, " son the decision is yours, I will stand by you and be there for you always. He just smiled at me, and said thank you mama and we took him home.

There was a large knot on his neck just below his ear that had grown so fast and was the size of a small egg. When the doctor released him from his care because he wasn't doing any more treatments Hospice was called in, he was already on oxygen 24/7. We rearrange my living room so we could put a hospital bed in there so he wouldn't have to be in a bedroom by himself, and it made it where we could watch him day and night. My daughter in law Carol was such a blessing to me. I don't know what I would have done without her.

When he would doze off we would step out and sit on the porch for break and smoke a cigarette. We would always sit where we could hear and see him. One day we had stepped out on the porch to take a break, and there were 17 butterflies that landed on one of my flower boxes. They were in a straight row just sitting there. There was some flying in the yard and one came and landed on Carol's head. We looked around and seen there were none in my next door neighbor's yard, or anywhere else. This was another sign for me, that Ray's time was coming to an end. I have an Angel Trumpet plant in my backyard and 17 trumpet blooms opened up, to me that was another sign. At this time the cancer was closing in on his on his throat and making it hard for him to swallow. The only food he could swallow with pudding, jello, or applesauce. We could get him to drink some ensure to help in getting his vitamins and trying to build his strength but that was about it.

Now the cancer was moving to his head. It was getting hard to understand what he was saying. We took his medicine and had to crush it up and put it in ice cream, applesauce, pudding or whatever else we could get him to eat at the time. Then he got where the only time he would eat or drink was when he had to take his medicine, because the pain was so severe when he swallowed. The weekend before he graduated and went home, Carol nor I wouldn't trade one minute of it. We were up 24-7 with him for 4 days straight. That Friday Carol came and helped me with him during the day and we figured he had enough medicine in him he would sleep through the night but OH NO he wasn't going to do that. I had a house in Clarkton that I cleaned the first Saturday of every month wouldn't you know that next morning was the first Saturday of the month. He was restless and had stayed up all night Friday night, Carol called to see how the night had went and to tell me she was on her way, I told her he stayed up all night wouldn't take his medicine and still wouldn't take it. Carol said I'll be there in a few minutes and here she comes and he takes his medicine for her. She stayed with him all day Saturday well I done my job and she told me he kept looking for me and asking when is Mama going to be home, she had moved him from the bed to the couch to the chair and back all morning. He was restless that day when I got home I gave Carol a break to rest but she was so exhausted she couldn't sleep. That night she stayed up with him so I could sleep and it was the same he was restless and he moved from bed to chair to bed again all night. Carol rubbed his feet and legs during the night and told him she could take the pain and swelling from him she would, well low and behold the next day Rays feet legs were normal and hers were so swelled and painful, she just laughed and told people be careful what you ask for, you just might get it. She never complained about the swelling with the pain and never once left my side. She said she sat there and watched him play with the remote to the bed he was in the recliner, she finally had to tell him that the recliner didn't have remote. She moved him back to the bed, sat down at the kitchen table and watched him play with the bed remote, he would raise his legs then lowered them, raised his head then lower it, then he raised his legs and head at the same time and Carol told him if he kept on she was going to have to unfold him. That night with him will always be in her memories, good and bad but bittersweet all the same.

Ray had reached a point where we couldn't understand what he was saying, couldn't make the words out. But I will never forget that Monday morning September 9th, 2013 when he patted the bed and asked me to come sit down with him. That morning he spoke just as plain and clear as he ever had and he said "mom I love you" and laid his head on my shoulder like a 3 yr. old child would do. and I held him for about 15 minutes and then he said "I've got to go mama." I assumed he wanted to lay down because he was tired.

His nurse Gloria came about 4 p.m. and told him he needed to make sure to take his medicine because the last day or so we couldn't get him to take it. He asked her, if I take this medicine will I die? She told him I can't make no promises, but if you take it and you die then it was your time to go, if you don't then the Lord wasn't ready for you yet. She wrote him a prescription for some more medicine that day and Carol and Robert went to pick it up. On the way back they picked up some pizza so we wouldn't have to cook. Since Ray was finally resting we didn't wake him up to take his medicine. We sat down to eat and we blessed the food, I had took one bite, and the Lord spoke so clear to me "go check Ray." I went and I wasn't sure of what I was seeing and I called Carol over and ask her, is he breathing? She put her hand on his chest and looked at me and said mama he is gone. He slipped out so peaceful I didn't even notice. But god is so good he waited until Robert and Carol got back so I wouldn't have to face it alone. Carol called Gloria and she came back to pronounce time of death, and call the funeral home. She couldn't believe how sudden it was she said, "I just talked to him 3 hours ago." Carol and I were so exhausted we were just existing.

See God had a plan he knew 8 months ago when he was going to take him home, And I went ahead and made his funeral arrangements. Ray graduated to heaven on September 9th, 2013. we didn't have time to grieve, we had to clean Ray's trailer out someone had already broken into it and stolen his guns, his laptop and some other things. He had left his land and trailer to his nephew. We had got the trailer cleaned out, the lights turned off, his vehicle insurance cancelled, and closed out his bank account. Carol and I didn't realize how much had to be done with someone died, we learned a lot of good lessons from this.

Bill and Terry Thompson where his neighbors, his friends and his extended family. He love them as much as they loved him. There will never be enough words for us to tell them thank you and how much we appreciated everything they did to help Ray when he was able to stay at home.

My advice to this world is to hug, love, kiss and tell everyone that's a part of your life how much you love and care for them because...... "We are not promised Tomorrow."

Bible Scriptures I Relied On Daily

- Philippians 4:13... I can do all things through Christ which strengthens me.
- Luke 4:18... He hath sent me to heal the brokenhearted.
- Psalm 126:5... Those that sow the tears shall reap the joy.
- John 4:14... Greater is He that is in you, than he that is in the world.
- Luke 1:37... For with God nothing shall be impossible.
- Luke 6:38... Give and it shall be given unto you; in good measure, pressed down, shaken together, and running over, will be given into your bosom. For with the same measure that you use, it will be given back to you.
- John 14:27... Peace I leave with you, my peace I give to you; not as the world gives, do I give you. Let not your heart be troubled, neither let it be afraid.
- Hebrews 4:16... Let us therefore come boldly to the Throne of Grace, that we may obtain mercy and find grace to help in time of need.
- Psalm 23:1... the Lord is my shepherd I shall not want.(" He is all I want")
- Psalm 27:14... Wait on the Lord; be of good courage and I shall strengthen thine heart; wait I say on the Lord.
- Psalm 91:15-16...(15) He shall call upon me, and I will answer him. I will be with him in trouble; I will deliver him and honor him.(16) with long life will I satisfy him and show him my salvation.
- Psalm 91:11... For he shall give his angels charge over thee, to keep thee in all thy ways.

CHAPTER 13

Robert Dean Norris

Robert is the only biological child I still have left on this earth. And I thought I was ready to deal with all I have lost, but I wasn't coping with it as well as I thought. One day the devil was having a field day with my thoughts and feelings and I grabbed Robert by the shirt collar and told him "You will live and not die, and declare the works of the Lord." You will live so that you can bury me when my number comes up.

Robert drives long-distance hauling vehicles delivering them in the North, South, East and some states towards the West. He will call me everyday several times a day telling me where he is or what he had just seen. I couldn't keep up with it all, but I listen as he talks. He calls me at night to check on me before I go to bed, and to make sure all is well. I pray for him daily because of the fear I have of losing him, and that fear tried to destroy me. I put Angels around him to protect him, and would plead the blood over him that no harm or evil would come against him. And the Lord brings him home safe every time. I am NOT driving myself crazy about his safety now, but don't get me wrong I still do the praying for him everyday and night, that hasn't changed.

By now I have already been diagnosed with COPD, when you add that to the long list of health problems I have it can feel your mind with "what ifs." He watched his daddy suffer with it, and it was not a pleasant thing to see. His dad would have attacks in the middle of the night, and Robert would be the one to take him to the hospital because I couldn't see at night to drive, and it was hard on Robert emotionally. I am on oxygen at night and have to do breathing treatments during the day. I'm living by myself so Robert and Carol had an alarm system and a medical alert system installed in my house. So if anything happens they will be the first to receive calls from 911, Sheriff's Department, rescue squad or the alarm companies. I know he is concerned about my health, and I don't want him to worry about me while he is driving. He has enough to focus on, because going 70 miles per hour or more on the interstate you can't stop a big truck loaded on a dime. Robert is still driving around from State to State, but I know in my heart he is safe and always will be with the Lord on his side and in his heart. And yes, he is still very protective over me. Sometimes I mess with him just to make sure he is still paying attention.

CHAPTER 14

The Lord and I

When you live alone you have a lot of time on your hands to do a lot of thinking, at times that isn't good for you. That's when I started slowly pulling feelings I had hit on a shelf in my heart and mind out. I tried to deal with them one by one, but depression slowly started to take over. The Lord would allow me to have dreams of my husband and children to help ease some of my pain. I was angry because I couldn't do the things I used to do because of my health, & I tried to stay busy. The only time I was happy was when I went to church, or was teaching Sunday school, or I was reading the Bible and in the word so deep that was all I could think of. The more I thought about heaven, the more I wanted to go. It got to where I thought about leaving to go home all the time.

I wasn't worried about Robert because he has a good wife to take care of him. Of course she would have her hands full because I have spoiled him. And she thanks me daily for it. I have been blessed, she takes me to my doctors appointments and would do anything in the world she could for me. Most mother in laws don't get along with their daughter in laws, but Carol and I have a great relationship. We are a lot alike in so many ways we wouldn't trade that for anything.

For six months I would eat, drink, sleep and talk about wanting to go to heaven, and everyone would sit and listen to me no matter how hard it was for them to hear. I had convinced myself that I was going out of here soon. After you talk about it long enough it can become reality to you in your mind and heart. In February 2015 I felt the time was near, so I would go to bed each night praying making sure everything in my heart was right with the Lord. I told the Lord I would see him in the morning. I did this for a solid month, and would wake up and get upset because I was still here. I had talked about it with my pastor and his wife, they are two of the children the Lord has put in my path that I didn't bare. They kept telling me, that they needed me and so did the church. The Lord came to me in a dream, he was walking through a wheatfield holding my sons hand, and when he got about 30 feet from me he turned my sons hand loose. The Lord said I will be back for him shortly. I cherish those precious moments of the Lord gave me with my son that night. I woke up and realized my depression and deep pain was lifting only God can do something like that. God still had a plan. He carried me when I couldn't carry myself.

If I had focused on the word and staying here, as hard as I did on leaving this world, I would be a Spiritual Giant. God told me "I didn't tell you I was going to take you to heaven, when you thought you were going." You wanted to go to escape the pain you had been through losing your husband and children. But I am your husband and I have put children in your path that you didn't bare to bring some joy in your life. And I realized God had done exactly what he told me he would. He said "you didn't ask for my will be done, you wanted your will to be done." I'm going to raise you up and give you a new lease on life. I told the Lord I had to have a purpose to keep going and enjoying the new lease on life he had given me, or I would feel as if I was just existing here. So he told me he wanted me to write a book to help me heal from the pain I had endured. I had held everything inside and people would ask how do you handle this pain, I would tell them "The Grace God." This book is written to lift up anyone who has lost a child or children, or a spouse, to encourage you and minister to you that you can make it and endure the pain if you keep your eyes focused on Jesus, and stay in the word. For faith came by hearing and hearing by the word of God. If we didn't have any trials, how could we grow in the Lord. I put my gospel music on, and it brings joy, and the joy of the Lord is in my strength. If I hadn't gone through these things how can i truly minister to others, unless you have been there you don't know the pain. My biggest desire is to grow more in the Lord, I want everything he has promised me. I want to be all I can be for him. God can take a bad situation and allow good to come out of it. And always give God thanks for all things, and even in the bad times thank him for bringing you through them. Let me ask you a question, if it comes to the point that your Bible was taken away from you, is there enough word of the Lord in you to sustain you? Get all of the word of the Lord you can, and all you get for it if the Lord tarries you will need it. I think the Lord daily for what He has brought me from, and where he is taking me, and a higher level. The more of his word I get the more I want, you can go as far as you want you in the Lord, it is your choice. God is not going to force himself on anyone, if he did everyone would be saved, you chose this day who you serve. I chose to serve the Lord and go be with my family that has gone on to heaven. What a reunion that will be. There's nothing in this world I want to turn back to, I'm going forward until the Lord calls me home. There is not a situation that God can't carry you through, for His grace is always there to see you through if you will trust in him. Looking back there is no way I could have survived what I have been through, without the Grace of God, and I am so grateful. The Lord is my shepherd, I shall not want and "he is all I want."

My loved ones that have
Already graduated and
Gone to be with the Lord.
They are so loved and missed,
I don't have to worry about
where they are. They are
with Jesus praying for me.

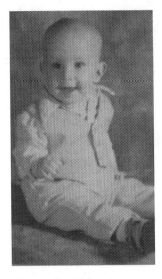

Warren Lee Norris
11 mth. old grandson
June 11, 1978

Ricky Lee Norris
7 yr. old Son
July 2, 1978

They were taken away too
early in their young lives.
But I know the Lord had
a more important calling
for my babies.

Warren Lee Harper

All grandparents are excited over there first grandchild, and we enjoyed every moment of the 11 months we had with our grandson. Once a child learns to walk, then they start running. And believe me he was a happy camper when he came to see Nanny and Papa. Those precious moments when they learn to love on you and give you sugar, but it was taken away to- to- soon. If we had only known what we were facing we would have taken more advantage of the short time, and that smiling face. He would melt your heart.

Ricky Lee Norris

He was one of a kind, with an outgoing personality. And seem to get by with things that others couldn't. I would fix his plate and put it on the table, he didn't like green peas. He would take one pea at a time and put his hand down beside him and was feeding the dog, so he wouldn't have to eat them. Until one day he got caught. He wanted his hair cut short, for his little blonde curls tickled his ears. I'm still thankful I had seven years of joy with him.

Rev. Herman Norris
Husband- 62 yrs. old
October 17, 1995

Teresa Lynn Key
43 yrs. old Daughter
August 29, 2007

Vivian Kay Jones
50 yr. old Daughter
December 26, 2010

Billy Ray Norris
55 yr. old Son
September 9, 2013

Carol Herring Norris
My Page To Mama

Mary Norris (Mama) to me. You have been a part of my life for almost four and a half years. There has been so many things I have learned from you. Everything to do with cooking to dealing with your son, to learning more about the Lord and the Bible. These things will never be taken from me or forgotten on earth or heaven. You are one of the people who took the time to listen to me when I needed to talk, cry and ask questions. You encouraged me to start singing again in church. I thought that part of my life was long gone, but you showed me it wasn't. You took my son and my grandchildren and accepted them as your own, not many people would do that and I thank you for that. I love you as if you were my own mama. I'm not saying we don't butt heads we do, but in the end we settled it. Not many women in this world can say they have loving a beautiful, wonderful mother in law that they really do care about, but I can. Mama I love you, you will always be in my heart and soul and on my mind.

Love Infinity,
Carol

Robert, the only child I have left on this earth and his wife Carol. I didn't lose this Son, but I gained a daughter. They are such a blessing to me. They live one and a half miles from me and if I don't answer the phone they come running. God has allowed me to see the work he is doing in their lives, and there is so much more he is calling them to do. Robert plays the piano for our church and He & Carol do special singing together and separate. I am so proud of them, and I thank God for them. I don't have to worry if the Lord will call me home to glory, I know Carol will take care of my son. All though I have enjoyed spoiling him, Carol has spoiled him also she has her hands, full but her and God can handle him. I love you Robert and Carol very much. More than you know, and God loves you even more.

Love Mama

It's amazing how God will put people in your path to be such a blessing. I met Mishele Kaufmann through my daughter in law Carol. She has an artistic and spiritual talent given to her by God. I guess by now you know I love butterflies. God uses butterflies to send me messages. I had Mishele to take my coffee table and paint the top and put butterflies on it. She painted the top and free handed the butterflies, and then painted them. The Lord give her a vision before she even started the project. The Lord gave her the #9 of butterflies to paint on it. The #9 in Biblical terms means, Fullness of Blessings. There or 9 gifts of the fruit of the Spirit, Love, Joy, Peace, Patience, Kindness, Goodness, Faithfulness, Gentleness and Self-Control. Devine completeness from our Heavenly Father is the meaning of the #9 in Biblical terms. Mishele walks in the gifts of the Spirit. She did this for me in remembrance of my son Ray that graduated and went to heaven 2 years ago. What a masterpiece, and what a Blessing! Thanks a million Mishele, and God Bless You!

My Pastor and Mentor, Rev. Danny and Laurie Rich. These are two of the children God gave me that I didn't bare. Through all the heart aches, pain, good days and bad days they were there to comfort and encourage me. And most of all to pray with me. Even the times I wanted out of this world they would tell me 'you can't go, we need you, the church needs you.' We need your prayers for the load gets heavy at times. I think this helped me through many of the rough patches and still does. When you pray for others God will heal you, and meet your needs. They are such a blessing to me, more than I think that they know or ever will know. Now that I have reached 70 years old they check on me often to make sure I'm behaving myself. On Mother's Day this year (2015) here they came with a rose saying "Mom We Love You" I want to tell them thank you for being there for me, and giving me the Word of God that I needed so much.

Love Mom

ABOUT THE AUTHOR

Some people don't have or know love, faith, or the belief or trust in the Lord. They did at sometime in their life, but the paths that came along in their life cause them to lose it. Some were strong enough to fight back and somewhere not. I was one of the Blessed ones.

I grew up a little barefoot country girl. At the age of 6 years I learned how to take care of my brother at 12 years my youngest brother. At the age of 18 I met the love of my life with two children and six months later we were married.

I live in the small town of Garland North Carolina. I have one living child left with me for the rest of my journey. But I don't have to worry where my other four children are because I know they are in heaven waiting on me. Even with all the trials and pain I went through in my life, the Lord has molded me into something beautiful of his own.

Printed in the United States
By Bookmasters